PAPERBACK POETS Second Series 1: Jennifer Maiden

TACTICS

Jennifer Maiden

University of Queensland Press

Published by University of Queensland Press, St. Lucia,
Queensland, 1974
© Jennifer Maiden, 1974

Printed and bound by Peninsula Press, Ltd., Hong Kong

Designed by Cyrelle

Distributed in the United Kingdom, Europe, the
Middle East, Africa, and the Caribbean by Prentice-Hall
International, International Book Distributors Ltd., 66
Wood Lane End, Hemel Hempstead, Herts., England.

Acknowledgements: *Arena* (Macquarie University), the
Australian, Australian Poetry 1973 (Angus & Robertson),
the *Bulletin, Free Poetry, Leatherjacket, Meanjin, New
Poetry* (formerly *Poetry Magazine*), *New Poetry From
Australia, Pocket Poetry Monthly* (Florida Press),
Poetry Australia, Southern Review, the *Sydney Morning
Herald, Westerly.*

*National Library of Australia
Cataloguing-in-Publication data*

Maiden, Jennifer, 1949 –
    Tactics/ [by] Jennifer Maiden. – St. Lucia, Q.:
University of Queensland Press, 1974. – (Paperback
poets. Second series; 1).
ISBN 0 7022 0944 9.
ISBN 0 7022 0947 3 Paperback

    I. Title. (Series)

A821.3

to Cecil, to my mother,
and to the memory of my father

Contents

The factory

Metal from metal, metal shapes metal
Metal eats metal, metal wastes metal
Is rebuked by metal, designed by metal
Metal rules metal. Metal pays me.
One thousand three times a day I kick
Metal and metal issues forth the same

    They say repetition enforces Truth
    And ritual is Divine, and here am I
    Queen of a chrome bucket
    That brims with silver-blue thunder
    Clinking as metal finds metal.

The green storm

Splinters of lightning
      Terse as opals
Cry from the green storm
Each fragment has a cutting edge
        Touch it nowhere
      Belief exhausts us.

The table

Soon the advertisements
Will not only shine but taste
       Conquering my palate
              as this slow brandy does
Savage, delicate, predictable

Were I not winter-hearted I'd respond
To any arm, its complex, hidden sinew
The involuted trace of lip & finger
The wrinkles & the unexpected hearth

I am buried in water
I float pure as glass
But mute as a fish I waver
And above me, under ripples
A wide shape quivers, suddenly
Transparent, too, & starving.

Branching death

passing a church at night

One must not beg for alternatives
But exhaustion chafes my mouth, my hands
   Are restless to be hidden.
My upright bones were made to itch
   Against the kneeling passions
 Here branching death
   Now blooms in nursery colours
Through orchard buds and wet grey violets.
Here, too, the sane are an aristocracy
   Polite, but dignified by absence.
The long stones wake as white as flesh
Below a bald facade of floodlit granite.
Alone inside a rector calls the sermon
His eloquence unlocked by privacy.
Losing his voice, my vagrant ear
   Abandons it: the timeless meeting;
The dead, the zealot and no listener.

Five nights away

in an illness

1

      The sky is as obvious as hunger
                Bare,
      The sky has no roots in man.

2

I've leisure now to see the clouds drip fire,
    The trees stand luminous, cruciform,
               Rigid with love.
           And I discern the angels move
In the debris of a soul
    Angels or some phantoms, far away
Behind the gallows' shadow in your garden.

3   I was asleep and you were here
  Behind you lightning
                Shuddered over burnt clouds
    You stretched and flowed,
              Blonde with leisure,
                A greed of beauty
  Beating my eyes with light.

4

The sun was ripe and fell into the sea.
  Ghosts of steam float
  In the thin bowl of coffee by my arm
Hiding the whole bitter tide of stars.

5

  The moon spreads sound not light,
    Whispering crisply on apples
  In trees she has frozen
      Star-severe, brilliant,
          Beyond our sly and mournful
            Darkness of tongue.

Climbing

This shadow at my shoulder doesn't shed
        The substantial night.
   The rope twists all breath
      From the mountain
        As simple as a bed
  Far above life in heavy wind you might
Fall beyond the common cliff of death.
With all my side and ear adhered to stone
There seems a place like hell to draw the dead
   Down so soft a body wouldn't wither
But hear the desperate lute lament ahead
    To lull the dog across a bloodless river

A prayer to Mendelssohn

Rich man:
Make me as ruthless to enjoy
A patience-wealthy voice
          as your quick majesty
Made peace within your powers.
                    Make me calm
Now to describe your smooth and logic joy
The supple cadences of air
The arabesques that strengthen a good journey
Without this gnawing sweat around my throat
Or sinew any longer tuned to fear
But prolix, mortal, vivid, help me learn
Your comfort, be convinced enough of breath
          To slumber in it, reckless,
                    whole as dream
And stir with hard cool eyelids on the dawn.

Shoplifter

When as a child he
Stole a china dolphin from a counter
He gave it to me, since
You cannot take a china dolphin home.
And envy as one may his sudden lust
In the bowels for a real china dolphin,
It was the symbol that I most admired
For an apple or a toffee there'd have been
A myriad of easy alibis,
    with hunger by no means the worst of them;
But there was no excuse for this, the theft
Was theft, the take was pure, the reason
Part of that great vulnerable Obscure
Of which he was composed:
Necessity.

Galatea

A. J. P. Taylor: "In politics the impossible always
            happens."

Remote the city windows
smoulder like full oranges.
Here in a deep
            & white labyrinthine
orchard kilns gleam
below a moon that liquidly avoids
the rough horizon. Pygmalion himself
is moist with senseless apprehension.
Dense in swelling silence,
                clay is climbing
habitual as bread, completely
understood.

Windheld the smoke trembles
gold in the gaunt orchard
& near the lolling fire appleseeds
enmeshed in greying blossom oddly burst
like fear from their crisp wrapping lace.
The bricks & sculpted anaesthesia shake
& realign uneasily, now searched
by hands of stove-hot clay.

Monk

from a detail of Giotto

The coveted exhaustion shakes
His eyes like quinine.
No high fear now, no gentle
Rind of light, but simply
The same unanswered
    gracile icon eyes, the same
            face smooth with knowledge
            and his mouth
a cool, creased
            ribbon of persistence,
Until the sour
    waxlight shivers through
                  his arms
        like threads of meat or wine
        and he kneels, tense again
To mutter comfort to his proven heart.

Over coffee

Inside at the green cafe:
A neon, as cold as a shark.
No other light. A soft
and sour steady voice explaining death
"That instant of nothing, it affronts . . .
the what? the strength
of every sliding victory
in my half-won struggle, snatching
at the sudden past . . . like
existential scissors, call it, shutting
on a private memory."

So sophist all true sickness seems
But, too, so naively alone
Unanchored by 4 tablets' rest from pain,
And sipping drama like a luxury.

Outside in the umber sun
Near car-tops the colour
Of cheap sweets
There are dolls behind glass
Reaching up to mimic trust
And bleating
With crib-cries made of tin
Their voices
Scratching like tinsel
Wrapping up
The truth, shop-neat:
Each useless, frenzied helpless memory
Chained back and fallen, fighting to begin
As a slow panic climbs and cleaves the surface
Floats tensing on the quietness of time.

Verandah

adept if careful,
we can still enjoy
our lax mythology of jazz:
its careless power
in skilful indoor fragments floats
unorthodox and comforting:
so dry against the darkness,
fighting
that cinematic subtlety of sky

(the spray eroded fences stretching
from here to the blond dunes are hiding
the gardens of the moneyed and the aged.)

night separates
in skeins from its weave
every whisper

and the doorglass dusks, nervy
with wind-woken lace

blackly,
the trees mirror rain
the skin
thins with cold,
the pulse
is blunt, uneasy,
real

(but homelight
                    still offers
its cleanest, apple taste
                    is cosy
with the dangerous charm of any
door opened slowly
by day, by accident)

from the raw ribs of the bay
a soft
but feral stormwind purrs
at our arms for harbour, sly.
despite the carpet,
our footsteps scrape like thirst.

(cold colours open
along our faces
                    intricate
with speaking:
the empty lighthouse —
automatic, dying — gleams/
gleams, remote as venus, on our eyes.)

Student

My darling has nurtured
in her voice a University
of NSW irony, that special
attitude, long research does impart
that crisp and killing
4-syllable frivolity to armour
one from bloody horror & this sort
                of party based
on sherry that dissolves
                nail varnish, stickily
(3 glasses), night & a sort
of lingering half-laugh
she has now, telling me
in esoteric shorthand: talk or tears

The poetry auction

Decide, decide, there is no space
To write this out again.
With cent-stiff face the virgin Time
Is bleeding out her monthly choice
Is warning in her mortal voice:
My merchandise is pain.

Silver wash-honey, hissing
Like bladder acid on the public wall.
Buy it & breathe like a hero.
It whispers, purges, succours, sings
It polishes your best eyes, brings
A knife-edge to your soul.

16

Couple

1

The dance in a second mimics
The helpless twisting head of love
As accurate as lacquer will allow,
The she
Drops laughter onto music,
Jabs her hands, aggressive
As challenged feathers working
                    rage into a song
And talks away his answers, casually
                    Is drowsy
                    & is listening alone.

2

His hair, dense with sweat
        Now wanders
In strands against the car seat
                    & the salt
Of torpor shuts his lips as he
Prejudges corners.
His eyes, young, sleek with noon-glaze
Prejudge her.
His gnarled hands clutch the wheel,
The fingers
Already eroded by gardens
Are as merciless as sleep,
                    avoiding her.

Quixote at the river

One could draw power here to make
More than a windmill tremble.
One could learn to hear again
The intricacies of breath, as casual
As the fragile spray, become
A fibre steely with complexity.
      One can already see, Sancho, that here
The ordinary light twists, falling
Like thick flashing water
              & one feels
The day's strange heat solidify our sleeping
Into a victory lost to the crisp shadows,
Upon the weary, autumn-pungent grass.
It doesn't seem Enchanted, but be careful.
He keeps such places for his battlefield.

Isolde & the censor

seen watching her at the opera

A censor — unfamiliar family man —
Applauds this antiseptic singer now:
Soprano-clean; a classic, safe Isolde.
He, deep undoubted dry well with a programme
Approves with a benign permission all
          His twin blades need not steal.

Sweet squabbling witches snatch
At randy secret music as they ride.

But reality grinds the rim of indignation
From my eyes with a diamond crackle:
Since abrasive as birth she sails,
                    graceful woman
Downstream in her glitter
The meltwater of glacial German
Appearing as pure reason in pure pain.

Tristan rants for Isolde
And every witch in me cries . . .
Not for love, no. That's too simple for these soft
                    and thirsty shadows,
Now searching for safe shelter in the night

The censor enjoys music but admits
In privacy, he finds it rather cold,
In this transparent country where his lack
Of privacy confuses appetite.

Isolde answers Tristan — & the censor,
Who claps, complacent Arbiter, not seeing
This singer is the smuggler of his danger
Though all the while
She carols the meltwater of her "heart".
                        My witches smile.

Hypothesis

A woman with a fine ironic face
There in the corner sits relaxed
and she
Is acutely in-love & acutely
              embarrassed by it.
The
Oblivious hero wanders
Like a legend
About the glowing pastel rug
Explaining a terse theory of McLuhan's:
That violence is the effort to create
A personal identity.
He pauses only when the lady sighs,
Adjusts her gentle hair,
              smiles, stands,
has cracked a tumbler softly in her hands.

A set of negatives

1

His face is grim here, with a short
White ache of afternoon boredom.
His bleak pretty eyes
Seem grey as wings, crisp as wings.
(His voice, then absent, was precise with terror
Of the wide world's casual death.
My tongue was on his numb mouth earlier,
                              both new.)

2

This is my first school: a real one
                    Predictably unkind
Note the grey eaves & brown rustic benches.
(Cicadas crooned intolerably of freedom
At lunch-hour teachers tactfully
Began to lock that gate
— you see it here, the milky metal lattice —
To hold me in there,
                    literally
                        hysterical & stumbling.)

3

And this is just a rock in the gnarled ocean
(A smeared stone stark as phosphorous
And cold with falling salt,
A souvenir
Snapped from the rusty roots of
                    strong sea lilies
Blurred by a sour & gnawing fisher's wind.
I kept it, since I slept there
            — after running —
Was wringing wet & still & isolate.)

4

This is a calm woman with hands locked
As if she were enveloped
In some furtive marmoreal prayer.
(She had hair like a cold yellow cloudscape
And found breath difficult. It was
At best an ambiguous intruder or
Some graceless & inexpert child, armoured
By patience & the usual camera.)

5

And here a mountain pony scents the lens,
Confronts it like a housewife with strict nostrils.
(& then she reared up, frantic, in a great
                    frail vanity of limbs
    & nipped the wind & flowed

Across the skidding clover to
        her secrecy of oats & tin-warm water.)

6

And this is just a girl: be merciful.
(The tall slow prisoner who swung
                        her secret fumbling hands
    Until
    They tail like comets on this negative.)
Be kind. (Her eyes
Are lifeless anthracite, & abstract,
                        terrified
Of course, but capable
In her last ruthless judgement of some first
        & necessary welcome within focus.)

Dew

Dawn is, in essence, sinister as fire.
A fume of birdcries
                    in the foaming shadows.
The black and omnipresent burning dew.
A leaf as stiff as jade, inhabited
By curt quarrels of light. The novice sun
As cold as an old woman's righteous mouth.
And soil, itself astir
With sightless unquenched grief to walk alive.

Roses

after wandering through a flower show, & recalling that
Gertrude Stein legend: TOKLAS: "What is the answer?"
STEIN (dying): "What was the question?"

"A rose is . . .
Second-hand roses
(poet's roses) no longer
apostrophised: known
already past exclamation.
After six days' bloom they give
like a frightened toad the smell
of all soft threatened nature.
Still:
The women clutched
a wind's spoil of them (blood-black
as widows, those roses) rather than
the alternatives: the rain-buds
(firm, dew-furrowed ponds
of cyclamen, sedate with youth)
Their eyes beckoned like thorns
— made thin with sun —
but sharp as if the self
was the only
defence left to them now
        & meeting them I thought
this must have been Stein's meaning:
                that the third
"rose" was a gloved question, but
this real rose — the question — seemed
odd aftermath of answers, like
a joke well-made, but thirsty,
        & departing. It was

doubly odd, now that I'd seen
those other women, like her, all
witty but dishevelled: cool
matrons in their way, who sham
intensity of peace inside
petalled shields, who go too soon,
too softly, so as to remain
unquizzed by the dark roses.

Fur

                        Golden
& invisible
in its own light,
the fur
tastes subtly of deserts,
immaculate as sand
it buries
her shadow in blond night

Ruthless
with boredom, she waits
inside it & imagines
the lonely dripping kill:
the fox: a heavy fool
suspended on a fence like Mussolini:
heels to the death-horn moon,
arms swinging.
            A flush of breeze
tatters his spilt pockets,
                    mottles
with frost
the open glitter of his eyes.

Her legs
swing from the tabletop,
waiting
to drop when a car stops
to hear it & stand
                in greeting:
a gloss of mellow scent,
life cut

cosmetic from best soap & paper,
kind,
she reassures by silence,
her first smile
quick as the vein that is harshing
beneath a fox pelt's sharp
                    & tiny
teeth of warmth on her throat.

Strawberry-bright

Steel snaps & stabs.
Strawberry-bright
& clean, the splashes
of blood deface the floor.
       Conveyor belts
slow to silence, & she waits
for band-aids, explanations,
            sticky tea.

I stare,
too deliberately, down
at the red on the workshop tiles,
remember other
times when she was bleeding.
Dispassionate, I think:
she ran, for instance, when she was
          a child, stopped
quickly on the Sunday road,
       was knocked to tears
by some slow Holden,
      & her mouth
rasped out shock, however brief.
& there were questions,
        & the blood
brittled on her hair like rust
(she showed it to me, later, as she
shivered in my bed, indulging
in descriptive luxuries of fear)

But when
did I begin to love her?
Not then, or when she cried
on finding the first blood
of adolescence (& lamented . . .
its sheer punctuality, I think,
                because, in truth,
that threat of the set future
was worthy of an hour's noisy grief)
                — I knew the terror, too, of course,
but children
never learn to love by sharing —
                so, when,
then, did the need grow out from malice?
Knowledge become more?
Why must I prove it now, as if
standing somewhere, looking
at a speckled floor, describing
blood drying, I am startled, so
sarcastic with relief . . . ?

5.00 a.m.

I build my eyes again
numb and bright and mortal from you,
taking

My words shiver with hauteur, an obscure pride
and pride is fear:
good measure of the depth a silence delves

I hide, as instinct tells us to, by watching,
where now the dawn's white alps
gleam on the wardrobe heavily
close to your empty waking hand.
My balance sways, there on a tightrope
I'm cold and frivolous with compulsion:
I must look down . . . .

(Autistic almost, one can't scrape on skin
the secret, public pleading: but time's fences
are wooden, rotting, always a sweat of splinters
under the hand's heel.
Darkness sways cool below, like rain.)

If at first sight the morning is iron
so at second sight it's bronze
and speed-gashed as stormwater,
quite strange, in fact, rebellious.
Such a sullen molten mould
seems furnace-wet, not ready for
pouring to your crouching shape of life.

Your hair has slept back into strands,
your eyelids open slightly, from the pressure
of shadows. Blue and white
their restless willowpattern gleams,
As always on such chaos any surface
seems tranquil with resistance to the light.

(As always, too, the changes
are insidious as rhymes:
        car, train, the remnant night
and factory-white girls, in colours harsh as habits,
lucky since the flesh will always linger
later in some easing grasp of loving
or for a stray caress on pastel lipstick:
our lottery, one accident
to drug or ache the tongue)

My hands, suave with their inexperience,
unclose to stroke your head's sleep-web:
alone, an indrawn universe:
its sun a spore of galaxies so vast
they move now without being.

(The radio. The news. The horror and the weather.
Lovesongs fight together, voice to voice.

They will theorise that voices, which aren't made
of protons and electrons, therefore may
be supernatural forces that are empty of decay . . .)

You say "How are you?"
and I answer "Good" while I am bad and breaking,
but some leaf blazes: an instant
of nova in the gusty sun.

To come to even that sad verity
is a thin beginning: pure,
and physical as grief, but small.
Again I enter here.
I borrow a warm mask from a cupboard, find
a stiff cosmetic odour which can burrow
into my taut lungs like something live.

(and "it don't signify . . . . . " if expectation
seems brutal beyond chaos: logical.
The morning's mosaic of habits may
have dead space left for me
to colour human, wry.
It takes all my odd rhetoric of life
to shake me out of sheets today, resigned
to daylight and machinery:
kinetic stars: but prophets which still fly
fire-slashed, and mock the flesh again
to comprehend its asking, though Pascal,
appalled for his solved heavens,
ran indoors from the sky)

Cocooned in loss, you turn "a second more"
to sleep. I grin and wait, but walk
your helix-printed carpet, watch
breath's weave flash unintended there,
must clench my fingers on my arms,
bruise wakefulness until it burns, and doesn't signify.

Tunnel

for Tranter, after rereading *Parallax*

A badger, tense with frost,
tunnels terror to peace. Awake
in thirst he hears
skulls congregate & bray,
sprouting fingers to caress
his armour into polished grief, until
some disregard of dark provokes
the accidental knife. His death just
membranes from the rock. Its astringency
snaps across his lungs. He searches
its tidespill until seawrack
shawls his wincing arm.
Gems & shells sweat fever, hold
hair, eyes, flesh in vacancy, & burn.
Blood-dried, his brain
drinks danger: he can't
concentrate enough to scream,
but the problem of evil drums: rhythm
& the drug of immediacy.
He shrugs: claws flex to earth again,
slash up, until they thaw by light
blood's liquifaction: time.

The usufruct

You'll continue, but must keep
your arms free to cope with strangers.
You'll continue. You will guess
there is a thirteenth man at the meal
who never asks a question, but
you'll accept your nightmares
as the operas of your exhaustion.
Meetings vote, and you'll become a king
to tense upon your mattress.
                    You'll go on
and learn to lounge on metal, praise
their moons and their variety of weather.
You'll grow. You'll own the foliage,
the dung and bricks, the limbs again,
the etiquette of power.
You will simplify yourself and trust
discretion in your bones to thaw
their year to harvest. Now you are
the thirteenth man at table.

The terms

Dreams bite blood inside my mouth.
I wake: *a nounless language.*
This room still has the wantoness of a truce
about it: paralysis in undertow.
       My eyes accept
A rug/ a vase/ but a tap hints.
I try to scowl with laughter
but I want the things to go:
          Not fear but nausea
& Sartre himself was never
more shocked by a clinging surface.
My arms laze where my finger
prodded fluff along the blanket.
Shadows — greeds for sleep —
contradict the semblance, punctuate
cries of colour. I'm not safe,
not sentencing the light.

Living room

Wine-tears grumble in your head.
Mad again in the kitchen — whole —
& as blonde as toast or health,
you crouch with laughter.
Your arms on the tablewood blur
its stain of dry liquor, which comforts,
as sweet as fresh humus, the dark.

An actress sees & shakes me,
vaguely: "More life in your hair,
than your face," & I nod
surprised by every compliment of anger.
The age that bruises your eyes
will blacken in my skin again, death's fete
froth caustic bubbles on the spinal nerve.

This is the raw loss, the earth.
Trust it enough to forget it.

Circe

        The rain stops.
Her gate's pink lichen of iron,
where hearts ripen on the vines with grapes,
dries like the scab from a fall.
I swing its maze of rust until
the heat stills my hand.

Her weird steep laugh:
so welcoming — but what? —
& an edgy whiff of sulphur in the hall,
perhaps from the floor polish, or her cat.

She always says "You trust too much
. . . you never will be told . . . "
"Well, no, but then my innocence
is purposeful: ignominious but chosen . . . "
I relax, with my sleek head
bent to touch the wood,
grunt into my handkerchief, scared
to be understood & broken.
I needn't talk tonight.

She'll watch
the saccharine whirl in her coffee,
never offer to tell my fortune
now, as she used to do.
I thwart her trade — which is to listen — too.

She still thinks that I should need more
than sex & pillows & a phenobarb
to satisfy my famine for the sea

beyond her garden & this ample trough.
One night again to calm her I'll pretend
humanity & lie it was a loss.

The metaphor

I memorize the tragic "ethos", stray
about your room. You protest in a fever:
cry out with plotless candour, damp as love.
                               I write:
"So mimesis means some comparison . . . "
the term's last essay, set in Tragedy . . .
As you sleep, I shut Greek books,
I stretch my silence so as not to wake you,
try brushing the rain's chaos from my hair,
try lipstick like a synthesis of blood.

You wake bewildered, stare
at storm-flux on the window, watch, afraid
some stranger there is snatching at your breath,
and hold me for protection, beg my help —
but my mind is too unslept to enter pain
or to quiet anything but details:
your face, the smoke-chafed lips,
the cords that bead your throat with age;
though at your door the bat-grip of a branch
shrilled on me with its claws,
air drank from my eyes, and the world
cut with a moon-raw brilliance.

My hands hug your wrists
and are useless. I say "I love . . . I love . . . "
all night so I can doubt it.
Studious of "crisis" I can hear
the murmur of the sheets, skin-subtle, smearing
your sleep with their starched peace.
Relaxing, I read, lulled again. Again
the fleshless winds wake, rocking with my fear.

Epidemic

in New Guinea, 1970

Astonomy glitters, gay on dark creation,
even here where fat streams gnaw
dense with plague into the yellow fields.
We won't be bruised by fear if we are angry,
but of the two — the sickness and the health —
I shut you in the first, you know it.
I took you to the coldest room, and loved.

We haven't yet confirmed our escape,
            and must convince each other.
What would I do if you ran to me in pain?
I'd struggle with a vacuum only,
you would be shouting out from death,
not horror. Still I stay here.
My hands are white as scars,
            and torn by caution
must ration out your blood from every well.

Reception in the garden

Her face has borne
its veiled absence,
smiles.
       She has knelt
& is frozen in the diamond

Now, candle-sleek, her knuckles shut.
Here, spindrift on plump bushes,
blown slack as steatosis,
the gossamer, the pupa
ooze into dry birth

Now, lion-faced, the leprous moon
snaps into its diamantée snarl
an habituée of impatience, cold
in her eyes that wait, alfresco
to lacquer it smokily, crisp
& stellular with fear.

Flanked creamily in matronly
rose-diamonds, her mother
retreats for better emphasis
gossiping on bulbs.

The husband is a builder,
                 smiles
at all he should remember, warm
with eucalyptus in this garden:
his wife's thighs, aromatic with his weight,
straining to come, but discreetly . . .
some bricks . . . a heavy dream . . . His heart

seems still sharp. His laugh
a weapon, flashes
defying the unborn

Haptic chess

*". . . the existence of two creative types, a visual type
which 'starts from his environment', whose concepts are
developed into a perceptual whole through 'the fusion of
partial visual experiences', and a haptic type who is
'primarily concerned with his own body sensations and
with the tactical space around him . . ."*
                  —Herbert Reed on Henry Moore

Hands are flimsy mongols:
hurt, will primp for pity, cage
fists in ivory.
"I'm half n' half myself sometimes,
             I need
the milk but relish cream," I shake
here into over-talk & into
under-knowledge so acid
it whispers like a liquid on the board

"the truth is rest, but then
old anti-self is ripe again:
you are alone & suspect
you are real, alone, & can
twist through the thing like a hero —
say, Bond in his undersea peril,
tested in tunnels by torture,
deep in the villain's design.
The danger of the dream's still that
it works, & that you find
yourself obliged to poniard some
dragon for its status, spend
a sharp, a safe, a dilettante mind . . ."

that warmed
& wilful sleep behind the waking gaze
won't prosecute the life
                interpreting
mouths flurried by each taut
insomnia as energy of moves
& architected obstacles in pawn:
    static as hate, it thrives
                    by use:
a tied unflurried shorthand for that
strain   black circles scream
as queens, the panic
too blurred to open, tears
freeze interface, exhausted,
            armed.

Prang

Lie on your back in the street
& feel the crack of blood
in your mouth warm on your chin,
& the tar-mud in your hair
                    your arm
on the flooded curb & the ants
using you for a bridge to the light,
to the burning feast of the sun

Musak

Pause a moment, rest & type.
Companionably here
a petted carpet breathes
somewhere of railway pastry, pizza wine.
Window-vistas bright
as a surgery hang
private in the living afternoon.
Their filmed branches fade for you
in the frisk & blow of dusk.
Pause. Powder down the slightest
freckle of opinion.
Smile for the compact corridor.
The pulse-neat croons still clamp
a nerve between your shoulders,
& the sensa of the threat can crawl
for filing, pacified.

Commercial

She sells: the tires'
   keen fingernail-screech on ice,
the moon-rapids on the road, her face,
the windscreen steamed with midnight,
            & wind-dregs
dank in her lips, new frost
choking the radiator like a snarled
spangle of hairballs,
              wheels
rattling like dices down the dark,
          her scarf
adding its slim brilliance to the breeze.
         You buy
if not the vehicle, at least
the formula, the ease, the fast
black & white of answers.

Mer-world

Victoriana's dancing, dry as daisies.
Here are butter-fat Palgrave blossoms
still sun-squat & embossing,
wind-honeyed as the bones,
the drained grass, the stained glass, the stones.

One contrasts that & the mer-world: they
sewed dry theory in it, but — God —
   the liquidly upholstered rationale.
Succesful amphibians. Darwin
& Arnold, I mean; many mermen &
the cloven hoofprints drowned.

All the lorn world lost & undersea

               oozing

               oozing

those salt tears from the tombstones
               black
the breakwaters of dew
& there the Heathcliff footprints: clay, the whole
   estrangement, say
of shelly pews & poor Tom trudging
   away to the little white lady
               Ellen of the Scales
                    shoals
Lot's wife with sand-blonde tail
   fin prints
             but sea of sea
Blue Mary & no more chimney

no lace or spinning jenny
great clocks or muscular
Xianity, only
        blood, & even here

now, half ghosting sugar flowers,
blood seems rainlight & is webbing
stemming & mossing, blown
as bricks that gloom in silhouette:
it is not
        air alone in which one waits
with its wet dusk taste of tin.

Dickensian, the dripping moon
clambers, lungless, lost, but from
the sprawl of barrier & gate
the head-high hulks of stone.

Lithgow

In rain's oxide fissures
    the ferns
star open-cut coal
its jetty teeth, a face
the bitten edge
in soot that stings
& bites all sunless
jowls of the road
the miner or the road
that licks & grits into
the stubby wattle, tars
each stubborn cliff
   the cut
each lifelong cinder
in the thunbnail a toy
for nervous voices fingers
ferns   wave veiny
dinosaurus stems
in coal on coal
from coal they grow
in appetite for coal as we
grope & drill for hunger
in our ancestry

Fingertips

On TV, the AM chef
is being fed. He warns:
"In bacon as beef
for the connoisseur
the fat of the best
        meat must
be yellow not white,"
or bloodful.
      Yellow, but
like used ivory, & taste
of sunny saffron. It must
be as spicy as leaves
       & warm
       & pure
he nods
as clean as a tonguetip
"pure"

Morning-clean now
an instant in leaving
I watch the screen
the chef is eating. Here
beyond the frost-gilded
        windowsill
the grass-phantoms thin back
inside the sun to thaw, as real
as the mucus of morning.
Ice from the wreathed
& matted birdsong
pools as my fingertips

gnarl,
       their flesh half void
& white on the opening door.

Mystery

"& if I don't take care
webs will thread in corners
anywhere"

                    Here
tan cushions full to popping
glint very fixed, with the eyes
of maniacal teddy bears,
their anti-flesh buttons
cleanable
everywhere
the apple-a-lilac curtain
dapples, breathy & contained

Money-spiders thread & hide
as day's emphatic suction combs
the dark side of the chairs'
dichotomy

Of your
decor
I'd venture, too
a Carter Brown description of
the sullenness of breasts, perhaps
the teeth the haunch the keen
tip-tilted pout of every bone
or detail on
    detail hint
at the sophistry of wrinkles
in the dent below your eye,
                    its own

down-drawn delta
on night-blue sheen of fear.
                No two
webs thread in your corners
anywhere

Slides

"There the Parthenon, & there
                    the cloud's edge withers.
There the Thames smokes
            the fountains prance
in reining wind & there
like a baked alaska
the opera house still curves
its blanched & clipped
magniloquence & sugars
the deadpan of an azure
                plate of sky"
At night we wander
            like late tourists
            through our own blood
            shining torches
at rats & swallows burrowed warm
            in antique porticos.

Tactics

1

Telling this fiction,
    finding the thing,
dressing one story
    once I would have been
defeated by each dying
novel of your skin.

"In its unspun knots of water
the sun in the harbour shows
leaf-embossed like a sideboard of silver
an antique's ominous glow.

commuting back on Sunday
to the ecstasies of sleep
two voices edge & flicker,
as one scar of cloud
gells in a dusk current
to bed the vales in blood.

irritation's pincers set
new flesh between her brows,
& the girl's moist hair clings, bundled
by her knuckles from her nape.
he listens as if gentle
& withdraws to concentrate
on her tired shrugs of walking
in the canna-rooted slime,
then glances down, impatient
at the wristed beat of time."

2

No, the last line rhymes too tightly,
& time's random spill is strange —
too anarchic to quite execute
immaculate revenge . . .

no consequence is needed: just
those waters & a wristed watch,
that world . . .

all histrionics prove
too obviously good there, like
some businessman who pensions off
his ghosts above the basic wage,
too desperately good.

love's Tory, too, I'm anxious, need to keep
my facade for your fluxing clay.
angled in my compact, powder-vague
& various as peace, you sprawl
on the tide-auburn shale: a wet
nun's coif — my hair — reflects
the crushed sun-cellophane sea.

"Don't hurry for me," you lounge
where mantled finches suck & brawl
like sparring flames, noon-rapid: tall
in fitful flashes, echoer
at ease to disconcert, you yawn.

"I won't keep you long now," I say,
         & though
I now can't keep you long,
         delay
that working of the world, to gain
Its expertise, a tactic of return.